FAITH HOPE and LOVE

by Alison Stedman

New Wine Press

New Wine Press
P.O. Box 17
Chichester
West Sussex PO20 6YB

Royalties from the sale of this book will be donated to
TEAR FUND

ISBN 0 947852 40 9

Printed in Great Britain by The Guernsey Press Company Limited,
Guernsey, Channel Islands

DEDICATION

To my brother Ian

We share the same parents,
We shared the same childhood,
We shared the same home,
We grew up together;
But most of all
We share the same Saviour,
We love the same Lord,
We are brother and sister
    In Christ.

FOREWORD

It's a privilege to write a forward to this book because Alison's story is one that excites me.

Alison first made a commitment to God some years ago but more recently she experienced a new infilling of His power through the Holy Spirit. It was as she felt His power in her life in a new way that her gift for writing poetry developed.

These poems are the expression of that God-given gift and the fruit of a life committed to Him. They are a reminder to each one of us that in His hands we will uncover potential that would otherwise be lost, and that as we surrender ourselves to Him we discover our destiny and come to understand how much He desires our lives to be filled with good things.

God has given Alison an insight into life, human nature and God's heart and the ability to express this in a thought provoking way.

I am pleased to be able to recommend her work to you.

Steve Chalke October 1987
Director of Oasis Trust

Contents

HOPE

LOVE

Faith

Faith

F ollowing Christ
A long unknown paths
I n the darkness of the world
T aking the risk, while
H olding His hand.

Resting Awhile

The hum of the city
Passes by my window -
London carries on
Rushing by,
Never ceasing;
But
His Peace,
His tranquility,
Fills my room
And enters my heart.
He says ....
Stop a moment,
Come to me
And I will give you rest.

Matthew 11:28

In The Beginning

In the beginning
Christ came to us
An unborn child.
Mary praised God
For her gift of life
And bore Jesus -
But
If she had said no
To God's plan.
Jesus,
The Christ-child
Would have been
Unknown,
Unborn,
Unloved,
In the womb
.... Crucified!

Luke 1: 35 & 38

Comic-Strip Man

Listen to Christ's words
As a child.
The man who talks in pictures,
Everyday language
To show His extraordinary love
To ordinary folk.
The parables of His kingdom,
In simplicity -
So that
His majesty,
His purpose,
Can be revealed to all,
Who believe
With a child-like faith.

Luke 10:21

The Only Begotten Son

A unique entrance
And a unique exit
For
A unique Son
With a unique purpose.

Acts 4:12

The Loving Cup

His cup of suffering,
My cup of joy,
Meet ....
In a toast of love.

His Body

His body was
Broken,
So that we
Could be made
One body,
In Him.

Forgiveness Unlimited

One death,
One resurrection,
Gives us
Forgiveness unlimited!

1 Peter 3:18

The Gift

Wrapped in a poor background
Of a persecuted people,
Tied up with an unfair trial
And a criminal's death.
Paper and string to cover
The gift from God -
Jesus.
He did all the work
And we collect the prize!
A strange idea,
Unfair you might say,
But God did it!
He gave us this unearned gift
FORGIVENESS
Through His Son.

Jesus Wept

Just two words
Speak volumes about our Lord -
A human cry
Human feelings,
A welling up of emotion,
In this
The Son of God!
Tears for whom?
Jerusalem?
The world?
Us?
You and I?
Who knows! -
- But for all of these
He still sheds tears
Today!

Luke 19:41

The Road Ahead

How You must have suffered, Lord,
Approaching the city walls.
All those people ....
Cheering,
Bowing,
"Here comes the King!"
A multitude
Of blind eyes
And weak hearts!
- You could see
That lonely cross
And the pain ahead.
Cries of "Crucify Him!"
Were to ring in Your ears.
Their hands lifted up
In anger
Instead of love for a King.
But still You went down that road,
Carried by the same love
Which surrendered all
On the cross ....
And it is the same love
Which said:-
"Forgive them,
For they know not
What they do."

Matthew 21:9
27:22 & 23
Luke 23:33 & 34

His Hands

Loving,
Healing,
Praying hands -
Pierced and bleeding,
Stretched wide,
To receive,
To embrace,
To forgive,
To lift us up
To the Father.

Isaiah 53:5

Scarred in My Name

On His hands,
His feet,
His side,
His head
And in His heart
Are the eternal scars.

Jesus,
Who put them there?

He stretched out His hands
So that I could see,
.... It was my name
That was written there!

Isaiah 49:16

Hidden in Christ

Jesus,
When You look at me
Who do You see?
- the leper who needs cleansing,
- the prostitute who needs forgiveness,
- the blind man who needs sight,
- the dead man who needs life?
Perhaps a part of all these;
You loved them all
And gave yourself for them all
.... and for me!

Now, Father God,
When you look at me
Who do you see?
- Only Christ crucified,
His scars,
His pain,
His blood
.... because He took my place,
My life has been hidden
In Christ!

2 Corinthians 5:21

Be At Peace

We pray for peace,
We march for peace,
We search for peace;
But do we really give ourselves a chance
To know peace?
Our days are busy,
Our minds full of 'important' things
.... but Peace ....
Can we find the time?
To be at Peace
We must -
"Be still and know that I am God".

Psalm 46:10

Peace

Your Peace
Is like sitting on the top of a mountain -
Looking at the view on a still, new morning.
Wonderfully breathtaking,
Vast,
Beautiful,
Awe inspiring,
Humbling,
Yet comforting.
Everything around looks so bright and fresh,
Clear and never ending.
Sitting there,
Just a tiny speck on a massive landscape,
We become part of it,
Part of the Peace which surrounds us.
Thank You Lord,
For Your perfect Peace.

Isaiah 26:3

His Peace

We do not have to strive for
His Peace,
Because He gives it freely
As a gift,
Through His Son.
- A Peace
Which we can't understand
And don't deserve;
But which we can just reach out for
And receive
In abundance.

John 14:27

Call This Number

Any time of the day or night,
Never engaged or out of order,
Guaranteed not to hang up,
Responds to all problems, queries and requests,
Answers any length of calls,
Listens patiently to callers of all creeds,
  nationalities and social status.
Understands all languages,
Heard clearly from all corners of the world.
Complete confidentiality,
Joint calls welcomed.
All promises given are eternally honoured.
FREE PHONE - The bill has already been paid
In full!
Just pick up the receiver
Of the prayer line
To God.

Philippians 4:6 & 7

Life's Music

You know all the words, Lord,
Because You wrote all the songs.
You put praise in people's hearts
And the music in their ears.
You are the conductor,
Binding the melodies together
And giving them Your life.
Teach me the song You wrote for me,
And never let me take my eyes off
You ....
My composer and conductor.

Psalm 34:1

Waterfall from God

I lift my hands up to You,
I lift my face up to You,
I open my heart to You,
And feel
The cascade of Love
Flowing from Your throne.
A beautiful waterfall of Love
From heaven
Descending
To earth.
Sparkling,
Pure,
Refreshing,
Water.
So sweet,
So clear,
Washing over me,
Cleansing me,
Quenching my thirst … and …
…. Overflowing ….
Soaking and filling me
With Your wonderful
Incomprehensible,
Peace!

John 7:38

Upward Climb

Why do we desperately
Climb up the mountain face,
Often forgetting
That our Guide
Has gone on ahead
To the top . . . .
And is holding tight
To our life-line?!
Help us to look up to You Lord,
And not down to the ground below us.

Colossians 3:1 & 2

Radiant Faces

God
Met with Moses
Face to face
On the mountain,
And his face shone
For all Israel to see! Exodus 34:29 & 30

Jesus
God's glorious Light
Transfigured
On the mountain,
And He shone
For His followers to see! Luke 9:28-31

Holy Spirit
Fill us
Transform us
So that we can
Reflect God's glorious light
And love,
.... give us radiant faces
And hearts! 2 Corinthians 3:7-18
For all the world to see!

Measuring Up

Lord,
Why are we always so ready
To judge others
Using ourselves as a yardstick?
Help us to see ourselves
With Jesus as our yardstick ....
Then we will see
How small
We really are!

Matthew 7:1 & 2

A Pebble of Victory

David knew
That the stone
He threw
Had God's mighty strength
Behind it.
- So even when the enemy
Looms large over you,
Your human weakness,
Plus God's mighty strength
With a mustard seed of faith,
Means
Undoubted Victory!

1 Samuel 17:47

Passing the Time

Time passes
Carrying all our tomorrows
To join our yesterdays.
Time walks slowly
When our tomorrow
Looks brighter than our today.
Then,
When the tomorrow we were longing for
Is here,
Time,
Snatches it away.
Time is so carefully measured,
But numbers
Can't weigh the value
Of time well spent.

Lord,
Through all the changes
And challenges
That time brings to us,
How wonderful it is
To know,
Of Your timelessness.

Hebrews 13:8

A Blank Page

Lord,
I ask You to fill
This blank page,
So that other lives
May find
The fullness of Your love
Lord Jesus,
And experience Your Peace.
Speak through my pen,
That from a few words
The way might be pointed
To You.
I will turn this blank page
Over to You,
For You to fill.
Amen

Hope

Tree of Life

My eyes were drawn
Towards the tree
On the hill ....
Standing
In solitude;
Branches stretched wide
Naked and dead.
Around,
A pool of red
On the ground.
Red blossom once
Had crowned its head.
A tragic silhouette
In evening twilight.
....
A few days later,
Early morning,
I passed by again -
The tree stood
Transformed ....
Magnificent,
Crowned in
Morning light.
White blossoms
Illuminated,
Weighing down the branches.

Sweet fragrance
Reached me on the breeze ....
I stood
Watching the sunrise
Over the hill
.... Then I knew!

Luke 24:7 & 8

Rainbows

What a colourful promise,
Spread across the sky,
God's covenant with His people.
A fine balance between
Sunlight and rain ....
Glory and suffering ....
Were you thinking of Your Son, Lord,
When You gave us the rainbow?
The new covenant
Jesus ....
The new bridge
Between heaven and earth.

Genesis 9:13-15
Matthew 26:28

Sunrise

Splitting the clouds
As burnt orange is injected
Into the sky;
Causing the pain
Of the long night to die -
To the beauty of daylight.
Arising with arms lifted
The sun's rays
Embrace the world,
Hugging all those silhouettes
Into colour again.
The hum of life .... begins -
Movement,
Colour,
Morning!

Psalm 113:3

What is Freedom?

It is not just having your chains cut off,
But having them thrown away.
It is not only having your sins forgiven,
But having them blotted out.
It is not just seeing the right path
But being led along it.
It is not only being held in His hands,
But being lifted up.
It is not just an escape from an old life,
But stepping into a new one.
It is not only a knowledge of God's Son,
But an everlasting fellowship with Him.
It is not just something given to a few
It's free .... so take it ....
This freedom is for everyone!

John 8:36

Jig-Saw Life

Piece by piece,
Day by day,
May Your image
Begin to take shape,
In the picture
You put together
Of my life.
You lovingly,
Patiently,
Slot each piece
Of my fragmented life,
Into the place
You know it belongs;
Until,
One day ....
I will be whole,
Complete
In You.

Ephesians 4:13

Christmas Eve at the Hospice

Happy tears
Shone on his face
In the light of the candles.
The soft humming moved gently
Past each bed;
A prayer for each person,
Each family.
Those old familiar carols
Told of years gone by
With family and friends
.... and now, time is drawing
To a close ....
But,
Today on the eve of new birth
We know,
That the Eternal Light
Shines on in this place,
And the Light of Life
Has overcome
The darkness!

Isaiah 9:2 & 6

The Race

"On your marks,"
Jesus died ....
"Get set,"
.... for me!
"Go!"
Come into my heart Lord!
The race has begun!

Jump into action
At the starting line,
And keep running ....
Keep running ....
Till you reach the goal.

No, you don't run alone.
Beside you, cheering you on,
Is the Champion,
Your Coach - for life.
Stop me tiring Lord,
Keep me on the right track,
Stop me from falling behind,
Carry me over the hurdles,
And train me to
Run beside you.

All who start the race
Can win ....
Reach for it -
Break the tape!
Yes ....
Everyone gets first prize!
The Gold medal
Has your name engraved on one side,
With a cross through it ....
And "Eternal Life" on the other!

Hebrews 12:1-3

Addict

An empty life,
Reflected in dull, unseeing eyes.
Existing only
For the next fix
Which keeps the tremors
And blackness of despair
At bay .... or does it?
That needle
Is only filling your arm
With false dreams.
A syringe of death,
Pushing the nothingness of your life
Further into your blood stream ....
Death is soon your only goal.

If you'd only turn around
On that long down-hill tunnel of darkness
.... There's a light!
A ray of love
Which wants to draw you back
To the living;
It comes from the man on the cross.
He stretches a loving hand out
To you - and says:-
"Your life is worth fighting for,
It can be beautiful.
Worthless - No!
I paid dearly for you.
I died
So that you could LIVE!"

In Your Image

We are like shadows,
When the light shines on Him.
In our lives
Your faded image can be seen;
- But we wait until that day
When we will be filled with
Colour ....
And in the twinkling of an eye
We will be made like Him.

1 Corinthians 15:49 & 51

Thinking about Forever

"Forever in my unfailing love"
- What a promise!
But I can't think about
"Forever" ....
My mind can't grasp that
Timelessness;
That vastness is beyond
My understanding and imagination.
The sky and universe is big enough,
Without the "Foreverness"
To cope with too!
But, if we could
Just realise
What the smallest bit of "Forever" means,
How could we ever
Start to understand the meaning
Of "Unfailing Love"?

Thank you Lord
For all your
Mind-boggling promises!

Psalm 89:1 & 2

Child's Eyes

Let me see again
Through child's eyes -
A fresh new world
To be discovered
.... everything new, innocent, exciting!
Teach me to marvel again
At the beauty of snowflakes,
Wonder at the first buds unfolding,
Dandelion seeds
Floating on the summer breeze.
To peep through the curtains
At twinkling stars in the vastness ....
As we grow older
Our eyes dim
Until
Only the greys and blacks,
The sadness and evil
Seem clear.
The world becomes too familiar,
God's beautiful creation
Overshadowed, marred
By the destruction of man.
Heavenly Father,
Heal our sight
So we can see again,
In your light
With eyes
As Your children.

Field Flower

Looking at the field flower
I see God's majesty displayed;
Woven in its intricate pattern
I see His purpose and plan,
In each soft-shaped petal
I see the gentle hands that made them.
In their bright sunshine colours
I see His inexpressible joy.
When the sunlight is caught and reflected
In a cluster of these flowers
How can we fail to see their wonder
And marvel
At their Creator!

Luke 12:27 & 28

The Himalayas

The morning light
  brings them alive
And they awake
In the golden browns and greens
  that adorn them by day.
Frost nestling in the valleys,
A scattering of snow
Gathered in the crevices,
- whiteness blending
With the clouds that shroud the tops from view.
These distant, majestic peaks
Shout to the world,
Pointing heavenward
  to their Creator -
You, who chiselled the mountains from the earth
And raised them up
To cut across the sky,
Towering above us
  in awesome splendour -
They reflect Your majesty.
As the sun sets,
The soft orange glow
Accentuates those craggy peaks,
And the dark shadow
Creeps down into the valley -
Until the blackness covers them -
Until the next morning
When they will
Shout again!

Psalm 90:2

Dandelion Time

1 O'clock

The green shoot pushes
It's tender head into the world.

2 O'clock

The sun and rain nurture it
- the young plant reaches for the sky.

3 O'clock

Strong against the storms
The buds begin to form.

4 O'clock

Strands of yellow unfold
Crowning its head with gold.

5 O'clock

Colour fades
- a perfect sphere of silver threads
replaces the petals.

6 O'clock

Waiting .... tall and strong,
Head nodding.

7 O'clock

Caught on the breeze,
The softness of time ....
begins to slip away.

8 O'clock

Tiny parachutes
Start their long, lonely journey.

9 O'clock

Travelling light
Carrying the message of life
Far and wide.

10 O'clock

Some never land
... getting caught up along the
way.

11 O'clock

Some reach their destinations
.... and are buried
to take root.

12 O'clock

..... so that new life
begins again.
Time has come full circle.

John 12:24

Wings of a New Creation

As a butterfly
Spreads its wings
For the first time,
To dry and become strong
In the warmth of the sun -
Lord,
Now You have made me
A new creation in Christ,
Spread my wings wide
So that the colours
You have given me,
Reflect
The love of Your Son.

2 Corinthians 5:17

London Rain

It's raining in the city,
Roofs become metallic grey,
Windows streaked.
A dull haze washes over
The distant scene.
High rise blocks
Stand like bleak stone rows.
Umbrellas fight in the rush hour,
Cars split the puddles,
Taunting the pedestrians with muddy splatters.
The city dissolves
Into a maze of puddles.

Why is country rain so different?
- softer -
Leaving the beautiful scent
Of damp greeness,
Instead of stale city exhaust.
Greens and reds, brighten;
Roses are given pearls,
Grasses - beads,
And each leaf becomes precious.
Country rain gives freshness,
New life -
- But in the city
Only puddles!

Jumping Over Selfish Puddles

When there's rain in my heart,
And water in my shoes,
He'll say -
At least you have water and shoes!
Only when I listen to Him
And turn from myself,
Can I jump over the selfish puddles.

The Web of Life

You know the plan,
The pattern is already mapped,
Each thread of my life
So skillfully woven
With Your loving hands.
As time goes on,
The creation is modified
To bring glory to the Creator.
On that final morning
The dew of Your love
Will hang as beads of joy
Reflecting the light ....
As a web
In the garden
At sunrise.

Psalm 139:13 & 16

.... *So Tired*

Lord,
I'm so tired ....
This week has drained me
.... no more energy,
.... no more emotion,
.... no more strength.
I have taken too much to heart,
- have been puzzling everyone else's problems,
- bearing everyone else's worries,
- suffering everyone else's grief,
So my strength has ebbed away.

Empty,
I come to You, now Lord,
To touch the hem of Your robe
For Your strength ....
To refill me,
Refresh me,
Give me rest;
Because
It is You who bore ALL our sorrows
Carried ALL our grief
On Your shoulders
.... And left them
At Calvary.

Thank You that now
I can rest in Your arms.

Isaiah 40:29-31

The Carpenter

The carpenter
Sits,
Head bent,
Hands holding
The shapeless piece of wood.
He is working
Patiently,
Constantly moulding -
Chippings fall at his feet.

He stands,
Wipes worn hands
And lovingly
Holds the finished figure,
Beautifully crafted,
Complete.

Jesus says:-
"Look,
I have been working
On your heart,
And have reshaped
Your life!"

Give Us Our Daily Bread

We need to come before Him
As poor men,
As beggars,
With nothing to give
But our emptiness.
We need to come before Him
With expectant hearts,
Hands held out
Ready to receive.
Our cup is empty
But
He will fill it
To overflowing ….
The water of life,
The bread of life,
Will replace our emptiness
With His fullness -
His Glory will be
Our riches!

Matthew 5:6

Love

The Precious Fragrance

She weeps ....
Tears of a repentant heart
Fall at His feet.
Eyes filled with forgiveness
Look down
At the bowed head,
As she breaks
The precious jar of perfume ....
He puts together
The broken pieces of her life,
And fills her
With the fragrance
Of His pure love,
Making her
Whole, ...
Forgiven.

Luke 7:36-50

The Meeting Point

Where could the Creator of the world,
The giver of life,
The infinite God,
The Almighty,
The Alpha and Omega,
Meet mortal man?

At the point of death ....
.... we met
At Calvary.

Philippians 2:5-8

The Sentence

The judge's hammer fell ....
"Sentenced to death!"
A gasp of horror and surprise
Rang around the court room.
The startled jury looked at the judge -
"But the verdict is Not guilty!"
"Yes", said the judge,
Pointing at the jury,
"But you are all guilty
 He is taking your place!"
The room fell silent.
The Prisoner said nothing
- and was led away
And crucified!

Isaiah 53:6 & 7

His Death

Jesus,
If ....
I had been there.
If I could have stayed with you,
I could have held up water
Instead of vinegar;
I could have eased your pain
With medicine;
I could have cleaned and dressed
Your hands and feet;
I could have taken out the thorns
And bathed your head;
I could have covered you
So you would have died with dignity;
I could have held your hand
So you wouldn't have been alone ....

But,
No.
Your death
Had to be
Different!

Romans 5:7 & 8

It Is Finished

"It is finished"
The sky turns black,
The curtain tears,
The barrier is lifted.
The sins of millions
Have been crushed
And pinned
On the one man,
Whose sinless love
Began
The end of darkness.

John 19:30

Recipe for Perfect Love

Take:-
The only sinless man,
One unfair trial of a love-filled life,
A crown of thorns,
Several lashes from a whip,
A jeering crowd,
Four piercing nails,
One wooden cross,
A cup of vinegar,
A scattering of frightened disciples.
Add a group of weeping women,
Two bewildered, dying criminals,
One dark afternoon,
A torn temple curtain,
One painful death,
An all-forgiving heart for a sinful world,
One piercing sword,
And a river of blood.

Mix it all together and leave it
For two nights in a borrowed tomb.
Then serve on a Sunday morning, garnished
With an empty grave, rolled back stone,
And a folded shroud.

This recipe has only been made once,
But the result is everlasting!
It is the most precious dish ….
Of Perfect LOVE.

John 3:16 & 17

Night Duty

It all begins at dusk,
When everyone is settling down
- except me!
We, the night staff
Like sleepy dormice,
Uncurl and head for the station.
Our pace quickens
As theirs slows,
The world is back to front
Or is it us?
Up and busy, never ceasing
While the real world
Sleeps ....

In their dreams
Do they see us
In the glow of the night lights
As we tiptoe past each bed?
.... but no one really understands -
'Night duty - oh what do you find to do?
Aren't they all asleep?'
You want to scream back
When that endless shift
Is filled with confused restlessness.
Their pain seems to grow
With the loneliness of the dark
And peace of mind sets with the sun.

It goes on,
Wet beds and vomit bowls.
3 am., an emergency admission.
As dawn breaks
And the tea trolley rattles out of the kitchen
The old lady dies.
Chaos .... screens around the bed ....
Phone calls - doctor - night sister.
Red-eyed relatives arrive
With the day shift.

"Nurse, where's my tea?"
Oh, the early shift -
It's good to see you.
"Busy night?"
"Yes" - they understand.
Report to them,
Is a stream of jumbled words
From thoughts spinning
In a tired, blurred mind.

With a pale face
And blinking eyes
You head for home.
Platform 5 is emptying,
People pass
Funnelled in the opposite direction,
You fight against the human tidal wave.

Doors slam .... reverberate through your head.
You sit and inwardly revel -
'They are off to work and I'm going home!'
.... and sleep
That wonderful haven of rest -
Until tomorrow
No,
Until today,
The same day,
When it all starts again!

The Traveller

He lay there,
Lonely,
Beaten by the disease that finally
Has stripped him,
Robbed him of the chance to grow old,
Leaving him dying ....

The doctor came by on his rounds.
Seeing he was afraid
'A bit up-tight',
Prescribed a tranquillizer,
And with a nod
Passed on to the patient
Who 'was making good progress'.

Then a nurse came.
Seeing he was withdrawn
But afraid of the questions
If she approached his fears,
Gave him a quick bed-bath
And busily moved on
To the cheerful 'popular patient'.

Then a fellow traveller came along.
Sensing the same fears
That he knew himself,
He stopped,
He sat at the bedside,
He 'bandaged his wounds'
By sharing his own feelings,
And 'bathed his sores'
By listening.
He 'put him on his own donkey'
.... so that now
They would travel together ....
.... until they arrived at the inn!

We are all travellers,
Some reach that inn sooner than others.

Luke 10:30-36

Storm on a Friday

It's Friday morning ....
Storm clouds hang low over the ward.
The atmosphere is thick
With the fear of the unknown -
All our doubts and hopes
Hover ....
The waiting is nearly over ....
What is the verdict?
Curtains drawn around beds
Can't hide the worried faces from us for long.
The doctors step
Into the isolated compartments
And each life
Receives a thunder bolt
Or
A burst of sunshine ....
Now they know -
Another Friday morning is over.
.... The storm breaks,
She cries ....
Only one woman this week
Has been given the label 'Cancer'
To pin to her breast.
.... One too many.
What will next Friday's storm bring?

Christmas Eve

Children's voices rise
As the excitement mounts.
Faces and noses glow warm
Now in from the cold.
Around the tree
Parcels of surprises
Receive eager glances.
In the kitchen
Busy workers
Prepare special dishes
For tomorrow's feasting.
Calm settles on the homes
As families gather,
To remember the birth
Of The Peace-Child,
Born in a stable
- the poorest of the poor,
Jesus.
Like so many today
In Calcutta!

The Mountain Children

Hot mists of breath
Cloud the window,
As two faces are pressed against the cold glass;
Gazing out into the dark world,
They sit snug,
Four solid walls
Protect them from the icy air.
Warmth and security
Are all they know ....

Somewhere out there
Far from their understanding
Are children
Whose breath freezes
In the mountain air.
Wind invades
All corners of their bamboo huts
- no glass windows
- no door to close out the night.

Children, as you grow up ....
Keep gazing out into the world,
But don't let the mist of contentment
Cloud your vision
From seeing the children
On the mountains of poverty.

Our Children

Children of the world
Your innocent eyes have seen
Too much suffering:-
You have held a gun
And suffered the pains of war,
You have been abused
And beaten at the hands of your parents,
You have been racked with the pains of hunger
And watched your families die.
The horror of humanity
Has scarred our children ....
- What an example!
- What an inheritance!
- What a way to treat
Our future!

A World of Difference

Our eyes met
And for a few seconds
.... Two worlds apart
Faced each other.

Standing with a pick in her hand,
And a sleeping baby tied to her back;
She stopped work for a few minutes.
Headscarf of faded cloth
Tied back dusty, uncombed hair.
Hands and feet leathered
From the constant work on the mountain road.

Snow lay around the shacks,
Icicles hung on bamboo walls.
A child was playing,
No nappy, no shoes.
Workers crouched round a wood fire,
Turned ....
And met our gaze too.

What do you really think of us?
Foreigners,
Strangers
From another planet ....
Called affluence
As we pass over your handywork,
Your toil and sweat.

She stared back at me,
How could I understand?
Not just a car window
Between us ....
A world of difference!

Ethiopia and Others

My heart and soul
Ache for you,
Starving people.
How can I ever imagine
How it feels,
The desperate,
Endless
Hunger?
Those living skeletons
Hardly,
Only just -
Existing.
Eating and
Scratching at earth,
To feed
Their scraggy, diseased bodies.
Thousands
Upon thousands
Of hollowed, pleading eyes,
- arms outstretched,
Begging for life.
My heart longs to help,
To go and give my love
- But it wouldn't be enough
To stop the hunger and the pain.
Oh Lord, my Lord,
Who suffered the most,
And who loves the most,
Help them because You know how.

Matthew 25:44 & 45

Suffering in Silence

Do you hear their silent cries?
They sit in the dust ....
Flies land on parched lips,
Dry eyes
Can cry no more tears
- water is too precious!
Eyes scream out
To be loved,
Did you say something?
Or has someone switched off
The television?

Matthew 25:44 & 45

Words

Words ....
Are the keys to hidden doors,
Unlocking a whole new world,
Setting the prisoner free!
They are weapons
To pierce the hardest heart,
They capture the strongest man.
They are tools
To build up the weak
And bring the proud to their knees.
They can express feelings
That the heart keeps hidden,
Becoming windows to the soul.
But
What anger can be unleashed by them,
Injecting the poison of destruction
Into so many lives;
While the peace of gentle words
Can bind the wounds of the broken hearted,
Quiet the troubled mind
And reconcile the bitterest of enemies.

My Lord,
Master of words,
Thank you,
That the power and love of your life
Is reflected in You,
God's living Word.

John 1:14

Walk to Nowhere

He walks
With dust in his shoes
And smoke in his beard,
Along the path to nowhere.
Eyes glazed over
With alcohol and loneliness
Seeing no one.
Where did you come from?
Where are you going?
Does anybody know you are here?
What happened in your life
That set you walking on this barren road?
Doesn't anybody care?
He gave no answer ....
And walked on
With dust in his shoes
And smoke in his beard.

Luke 19:10

Missed Opportunity

"Can you spare a minute?"
Holding a clipboard
With bright eyes and an enthusiastic smile
He questioned me
About things hypothetical
For studies of the mind.
I should have told him
About the fact
That Jesus loves him.
He recommended a book
By a man who has studied the mind
Through others.
I should have recommended The Book
By a loving God
Who created the mind
And loves individuals for themselves.
But - in weakness,
In self-conscious shyness,
My heart was deaf
My mouth was dumb -
Not sharing the answers
To the real questions he asked.
So I left him
With scribble on paper and an empty heart.
The yawning sinking in my stomach
The ache in my heart
Told me,
I had missed the opportunity
To share Your love, Lord -
I'm sorry I denied You
By my silence!

Rainbow Treasure

What lies at the end of the rainbow?
I don't see any pots of gold.
That bridge
Of many colours,
Like Joseph's coat
Is only a covering,
A symbol
Of the true worth.
The spectrum
Of beauty and light -
God's love
- the full range.
There is no end to a rainbow
Or
To God's love!
A treasure
Of infinite worth.

Borrowed Time

Time,
Like the hour glass
Is running out.
The sand sinks
As grains
Fall through space.

The human race
Is guilty,
By rejecting God's Love;
Falling .... away from Him,
With every second,
Every tick,
Every swing of the pendulum.
He waited ....

He gave us time,
At the eleventh hour
He sent His Son,
Who, took on Himself
The guilt of the world.
The judgement has been made,
The sentence was
Death ....

Jesus died.
Time stood still ....
He rose from the dead
- The clock has been turned back ....
He has given us
Our last chance.

But
When the clock strikes
Midnight ....
And Christ returns,
Will you be there?
.... Or will you be
Too late?!